Outgrowing the Pain:

A Book for and about
Adults Abused as Children

Outgrowing the Pain:

A Book for and about
Adults Abused as Children

Eliana M. Gil, Ph.D.

Launch Press
P. O. Box 40174
San Francisco, California 94140

Illustrations: Sally Haskell
Cover Photo: Dennis Gray
Editing & Lay-out: Wendy Jung
Cover Design: Diane Lozito

Gil, Eliana *"Foster Parenting Abused Children"*
National Committee on the Prevention of Child
Abuse, Chicago, Ill., 1980.

Gil, Eliana *"The California Child Abuse Reporting
Law: Issues and Answers for Mental Health
Professionals"*, State Office of Child Abuse
Prevention, State Department of Social Services,
Sacramento, Ca 95814, 1983.

In process:

Gil, Eliana *Reversing Dangerous Life Patterns:
A Handbook of Issues and Strategies for Working with Abusive, Neglectful or Incestuous
Families and Individuals,* Launch Press, June,
1985.

Launch Press
P. O. Box 40174
San Francisco, California 94140

ISBN 0-9613205-0-8

Library of Congress No. 83-82956

*To Carolita
with admiration and affection*

Table of Contents

Introduction

As a therapist, I have seen many clients who have sought help for a variety of problems including finding or keeping jobs, problems with a drinking or abusive mate, depression, general disatisfaction with life, or a feeling of *"wandering"* without clear direction or goals. When I inquired into their pasts, physical, sexual, emotional abuse and/or neglect often had occurred. I began to recognize similar patterns and difficulties in victims of past or current abuse.

I began running groups for adults abused as children, and the issues which arose and were discussed further substantiated some of my initial impressions. It is to the individuals who participated in these groups that I dedicate this book. They helped me gain insight and understanding of their current problems and struggles by allowing me to know their thoughts, feelings, perspectives, and pasts. They touched me and inspired me. They never ceased to amaze me with their unique survival instincts and strengths. They possess a special kind of courage that both permits and helps them to set off on a very long journey towards self-acceptance.

The information contained in this book is a result of my interactions with Terry, Joanne, Beverly, Susan, Laura, Maureen, Howard, Bill, Gladys, Lois, Carolita,

1

Leah, Nancy, Noreen, and Chris. I am grateful to them for reviewing the drafts of this book, and making thoughtful suggestions.

Other people helped with this project. Diane Lozito prepared the cover and generally encouraged my pursuit of this project offering her advertising and artistic talents along the way. Wendy Jung, owner of Letterperfect, edited my work and was in charge of the production including typesetting, graphic layout, and design. She brought her high standards to this book.

Christine Lines co-facilitated some of the groups, constantly contributing in her own unique style. Dr. Karen Saeger, Co-Director of the Redwood Center where I work, supports and encourages me. Most importantly, she believes I have something to say and offer. Dr. Saeger reviewed the manuscript and made many excellent comments and suggestions. I trust her with my life and my rough drafts. My thanks to Kathy Baxter-Stern, Executive Director of the San Francisco Child Abuse Council, where I also work. She provides me with spoken and unspoken support in all my endeavors, and helps create the kind of work environment where my creativity and range of interests can be pursued. I am very fortunate to be surrounded by friends at both work settings who inspire me and cheer me on. My appreciation goes to Dr. Robert Green, Mary Herget, and other staff members at the Redwood Center. Thanks to Elayne Savage, Laura Grandin, and Norma Sullivan who gave of their time and talents to the manuscript development. A closing expression of gratitude goes to my husband, John, who has been excited and tired with me throughout this process, and who has extended a helping hand just at the right moment. I always have to thank my kids, Teresa, Eric, and Christy because they like the kind of mom I am, and are almost always very understanding when I hide out to work.

IS THIS BOOK FOR ME?

Do you think you're crazy?

Do you think you're bad?

Do you have trouble finding friends, lovers, acquaintances?

Once you find them, do they dump on you, take advantage of you, or leave?

Are you in a relationship you know is not good for you? Are you getting beaten up? Does your partner drink too much?

Are things okay sometimes, but never for long enough?

Are you always doing for others, but finding no one returns the favor?

Are you distrustful and afraid of others?

Are you suspicious, resentful, angry at others, often explosive? Do you find others are always taking their anger out on you?

No matter how many good things others tell you, do you end up thinking they are lying to you?

Would you rather stay home alone, and lonely, than face people you don't know, who may not like you?

5

Are you still trying to figure out what you want to do when you grow up? Do you sometimes feel that you'll never grow up?

Do you have a terrible relationship with your parents, feeling bad around them all the time? Or do you constantly make efforts to please them, never feeling like you succeed?

Do you let people go on too long doing or saying something that distresses you before stopping them, and later find that you resent them?

Do you think you're good for nothing?

Are you drinking too much, eating too much, or trying to numb your pain with drugs of any kind?

Do you find yourself being abusive to your kids, or afraid to have kids for fear that you'll beat them?

Everyone has some of these feelings some of the time. But adults abused as children can have *many* of these patterns to extreme degrees.

Some people think they were not abused as children because they were never hospitalized, it only happened once, their parents didn't mean it, or didn't know better, or other people had it much worse. Abuse of any kind: verbal, physical, sexual, emotional or neglect, affects children. The after-effects can show up immediately or later in life.

Because abuse in one's past is difficult to admit, many of you may never have made the connection between what happened to you as a child, and some of your current problems. It's an important connection to make, and it will frequently enable you to get unstuck and move on to accomplish some of the things you want.

Purpose of this Book

This book is not going to solve your problems completely. But it *will* help you explore the questions, *"Was I abused as a child?" "Has the abuse affected my life negatively?" "Am I doomed?"* This is an optimistic book. It emphasizes the importance of the past as well as the present and the future. It will help you sort out what was, what is, and what can be.

This book will outline some of the ways you may have been affected by any form of child abuse or neglect. It will also help you to recognize the changes that can be accomplished in breaking patterns and habits which resulted from the impact of abuse.

Abused children learn by their experiences to expect little of themselves and others. They are not usually taught to trust, and end up seeing themselves as bad, crazy, and unworthy of love or attention. Just as abused children learned to see themselves this way, they can learn to adopt more positive ways of viewing themselves and others.

Who Is This Book For?

This book is for any adult who was abused as a child, or witnessed abuse in his/her family, and is trying to make some sense of his/her experience. It is also for professionals who help others (mental health workers, alcoholism counselors, teachers, etc.). As child abuse continues to be recognized as a major concern, more and more adults abused as children need someone to listen to them and help them sort out their experiences and the powerful after-effects.

"More and more adults abused as children are looking for someone to listen to them..."

This book has more questions than answers. I ask the reader to explore slowly the issues of abuse in the past. Seek help from friends, relatives, or counselors in order to fully understand the abuse, to put it in perspective, and to move on to a healthier way of relating in the world.

chapter two

COMING TO TERMS
WITH ABUSE AS A CHILD

Denial

Because you have started to read this book, you have taken a step toward exploring the possibility that you were abused, or witnessed abuse, as a child. Most adults abused as children have an initial period when

"Children who are abused begin to build walls ... and may be fearless.

they cannot decide if they fall into the *"abused"* category. The reason for this is that adults usually have a defense mechanism called *denial* that protects them from anything that is too painful. Denial helps block out unpleasant, painful memories. Children who are abused build a protective wall of denial which helps to keep them safe from the pain they expect or experience. By the time they are adults, the walls that protect them are very strong and tall.

Not everyone has a wall. Some children use other defenses and can appear fearless as if nothing bothers or touches them. If you were this kind of child, you may find it harder to acknowledge your hurt. I hope you peek at this book anyway.

"start lowering your wall, one brick at a time ..."

If you were one of the children who built walls, as you read this book, you may find holes in your wall. You may even find it useful to make an effort to start lowering your wall, one brick at a time. It's important to lower the wall slowly. If you feel unprotected and unsafe, you might become frightened. The wall has kept you safe from some hard truths all these years.

It's hard to acknowledge being abused as a child because in doing so, you also admit that your parents were wrong, or not perfect. *"Honor thy mother and father"* is a very strong lesson, and seeing your parents as abusive may feel like a betrayal of them.

As children and adults, most of us want to believe the best of our parents. They are very important to us. If we have a choice between whether *we* are bad, or *they* are bad, we are likely to choose ourselves. We might think something they are doing is wrong, but probably we will make up all kinds of excuses for their behavior.

Most abused children grow up thinking that the abuse occurred because of themselves: *I* did something wrong, *I* deserved what *I* got, *I* needed to be straightened out.

It is important to realize that everyone's parents and children have positive and negative aspects. If your parents emphasized only the badness, they did not help you to identify those qualities necessary for building positive self-esteem. It may have been that they had no idea how to raise a child, or were angry

13

and frustrated at other people. For whatever reason, whether you were neglected or abused physically, sexually, or emotionally, **it was a problem with your parents, not with you.**

Definitions of Child Abuse

The first child abuse reporting law was written in 1964. Before that time, certain behaviors were not legally labelled *"abuse"* and were not against the law. The definitions of child abuse have expanded over the years. For example, in the last six years, sexual abuse, sexual exploitation, and child pornography have been recognized as serious and prevalent issues. *"Child abuse"* is a term that lots of people use these days. Some of you wonder, if *you* were abused, why no one did anything about it when you were a child.

When you were growing up, child abuse was probably not openly discussed. It is not that it did not happen then, it is just that the definitions had not yet been developed clearly. Professionals and the public were largely unaware of abuse, and no one knew exactly how to deal with the problem when it was identified. Denial is not a defense used only by abused children. Society at large has had a hard time believing that children are abused by parents and that they need protection. You are not alone behind a wall. Your parents, teachers, doctors, and others may have had the same desire to hide and avoid the truth.

In addition, many abused children were told not to talk about what went on outside their home. You may have sensed abuse was not something to talk about or maybe you didn't know it was unusual. You may have felt disloyal to the family, or fearful of getting your parents or yourself in trouble if you told anybody what was going on. Even if you did talk, people might have felt that they shouldn't butt in, or perhaps they didn't know what to do. Because no one stopped what was going on, you may have been more convinced that nothing unusual or unacceptable was happening.

"Sometimes children are told not to tell anyone. Other times, although the threat is not spoken, it is implicit."

These are the types of child abuse which currently must be reported to the authorities by most professionals:

Physical abuse is when you are hit, pushed, whipped, bitten, punched, slapped, or burned, resulting in injuries that are left on your body. Some of these injuries such as scratches, burns, bruises, and welts, are visible. Others are internal, such as broken bones, fractures, or hemorrhaging.

Sexual abuse is when any person, adult, or child, forces, tricks, threatens, or coerces a child to have *any* kind of sexual contact with him/her. Showing children pornographic pictures or films, or telling them explicitly sexual stories can be a form of sexual abuse. Touching children inappropriately can be sexual abuse. Some children are forced or encouraged to have sexual intercourse with parents, uncles, grandparents, or friends of the family. Other children have sexual contact with strangers.

Neglect is when a parent does not feed a child or provide the basic necessities such as clothing or shelter, or medical attention if needed. Leaving a child alone when the child is not yet ready to care for him/herself is neglectful since it leaves a child in a potentially dangerous situation.

Emotional neglect is when parents don't take an interest in their child, and do not talk to or hold and hug the youngster, and are generally emotionally unavailable to the child. Alcoholic parents are often neglectful of their childrens' needs. Although emotional neglect or abuse may not leave physical scars, it has serious consequences for the child.

Cruel and unusual punishment is another form of abuse. These are punishments which are extreme and inappropriate to a child's age and ability to understand. Locking a child in a closet, forcing a child to be toilet trained at 4 months, making a child duck-squat for hours — all are examples of extreme punishment.

Corporal punishment resulting in injuries is also abuse. Corporal punishment is physical discipline and includes excessive spanking, kicking, or whipping which results in injuries. Spanking can become child abuse when it is done in an out-of-control way, with enough force to leave injuries. Using instruments to hit, spanking with a closed fist, hitting very young children, and hitting in vulnerable areas (face, head, stomach, back, genitals) can increase the likelihood of corporal punishment becoming child abuse.

Mental suffering occurs when a child is psychologically abused. If a parent calls a child names, constantly belittles the child, blocks every effort on the part of the child to accept him/herself, this can cause mental suffering to the child. Threat of abandonment can also make the child anxious and afraid, and is another form of mental suffering.

All forms of abuse are serious and affect the child. Children may react differently at different times. A three year old child who is sexually abused, for example, may appear quite

healthy yet express confusion or difficulties when s/he turns 13 and puberty emerges.

Minimizing

"It wasn't all that bad"

If you begin to think that you were abused as a child, you may have a tendency to minimize what happened to you. *"I only got beaten every other week"* or *"I only had to be hospitalized once."* Adults abused as children may compare themselves to other... *"I was **only** beaten; I couldn't have handled incest,"* or *"he only* fondled my breasts and threatened or scared me." **It's very important for you to understand that all types of abuse are important on an individual basis. The crucial aspect of the abuse is not what occurred, but what impact it had on you, how you explained it to yourself and others, and how it has affected your life.**

As you remember your past, you see it with adult eyes. It's hard to recall what your reactions were as a child. It's easy to look back now and tell yourself, *"It was OK."* But as a child, you may have suffered through hours, days, weeks, and months of fear or pain, with a never-fulfilled desire to please, to be safe, and to be loved.

"Remember as you look at your past, you are looking with adult eyes..."

Rationalizing

"They had too many kids, no help"

After minimizing, you may also begin to make excuses for your parents or explain reasons why the abuse occurred. Even though some of these reasons may be relevant, it is important not to let those thoughts interfere with the crucial task of accepting that the abuse *did* indeed happen and did indeed hurt you.

It is probably true that your parents did the best they could, that they were possibly under many pressures, and that little help was available to parents when you were growing up. It may also be true that they were abused, and simply repeated what they learned as children.

In some cases, abusive parents may have had emotional problems, or a drinking problem so serious that they could not take responsibility for their actions. Perhaps they were neglectful or abusive only when they were drunk.

It is important not to use these reasons as excuses that get your parents off the hook and keep you feeling responsible. There are no excuses for abusing a child. The reasons are important, but they never excuse the actions.

"It may also be that they were abused, and were repeating what they learned as children."

Selective Memory
"I know it happened, it's just hard to remember."

Go slowly as you try to remember the abuse. For many of you, this will be a painful process. You may have pushed the memories back so far that you think they are gone. But every now and then, you may be bothered by a memory of a particular moment in time. This is like watching a movie in which scenes of your life suddenly appear. It may be the look in your mother's eyes when she first took a strap to you or your father's eyes as he put your hand on his penis. These flashbacks are your memories trying to push their way into your reality. Unless you look at these scenes, make some sense of them, understand or accept them, the memories may feel frighteningly out of your control, popping up at the strangest times.

A useful thing to do (preferrably with the help of a therapist) is to begin slowly to allow the memories to come up and out. As the scenes become more clear in your mind, and as you remember more and more, you can begin to see what actually did happen, and you can clarify your feelings about the experience and see in what way those memories and events affect you presently. Some people don't want to remember because they think they were to blame - they caused the abuse. Some victims believe they could and should have stopped what happened to them, and are consumed with guilt. The purpose of going back this way is not to dwell on pain or to attribute all your current difficulties to these events, but to deal with vague memories and feelings in a constructive way so you are no longer held back by them. You may find yourself wanting to get away from these negative or painful thoughts. You may move on to other memories in your life which give you more pleasure. This is a natural response. Both kinds of memories are useful to you.

"A useful thing to do (preferrably with a therapist) is to slowly begin to allow the memories ..."

chapter three

OK, I BELIEVE IT,
NOW WHAT?

Anger

Anger is a very common response to accepting the fact that you were an abused child. You may feel you have been violated, betrayed, exploited, and unjustly treated. You may find yourself saying repeatedly, *"Why me?"* All the empathy you previously had towards your parents may disappear, and you find yourself casting judgments in their direction. You may want to hurt them in order to pay them back. Feeling angry is natural; you have a right to feel angry. Expressing this anger is the most important lesson to be learned. How do you get rid of all the poisonous, furious feelings you have without hurting yourself or others?

If you don't know how, you are not alone. There are many people who have never been taught what to do with their anger. For the most part, anger is seen as a *"bad"* emotion. Temper tantrums in children are usually controlled, and when someone gets angry and shouts, they are thought to be overly emotional and immature.

If you were abused as a child, you probably had violent, destructive examples of how to be angry. You, more than others (who were not exposed to abuse), must learn constructive ways to express anger so you don't end up exploding, hitting, or making yourself sick by turning the anger inward.

The flip side of anger is helplessness. This feeling of helplessness can quickly turn into anger or rage.

"The flip side of helplessness is anger."

Ask yourself *"What am I feeling helpless about?"* rather than *"Why am I so angry?"* If you can't find a quick answer, keep asking. Then, try to re-gain control (power) over the situation. To do this, some kind of action is usually required. Once you regain the power, your sense of helplessness decreases or disappears altogether.

Anger can be a problem if you find yourself on the receiving end of it. Because you witnessed

violent anger, you expect all arguments or expressions of angry feelings to result in violence. This is simply not the case. Many of you grew up without a middle ground for expressing anger - it was either not expressed, or exploded into violence. A middle ground is safe anger expression. (See Chapter VI).

"It is important to remember that friends often want the opportunity to help you..."

Many adults abused as children feel they cannot turn to others when they are feeling sad. They are either afraid to *"burden"* others, be rejected, or they may have learned that showing feelings gets them into more trouble. It is important to remember that friends often want the opportunity to help you, and although scary at first, you may find yourself getting what you need from others. **And liking it!**

Fear

As the memories of abuse are examined, you may suddenly find yourself feeling unsafe and fearful again. A certain amount of this is a normal response to geting in touch with painful memories, but if it persists or prevents you from leading a normal life, consult a professional.

Shame

Shame is another typical response to remembering the abuse and accepting yourself as a previously abused child. You may feel embarrassed to tell others thinking that you are somehow defective or that you came from a disturbed family. As you begin to accept that you were not responsible for the abuse, and that your parents had a problem many people have, you may feel less embarrassed.

Relief

Finally, you can talk about it! Many adults abused as children have felt alone in their suffering for years. They learned to keep their thoughts and memories to themselves. Accepting the truth, as well as talking about it with others, can bring a deep sense of relief. **It is as if energy, previously spent on keeping a secret, is suddenly freed up to apply elsewhere and to pursue more positive changes.**

—c h a p t e r   f o u r—

AFTER-EFFECTS OF ABUSE

DIFFICULTIES WITH TRUST
"If I don't talk, they won't get mad."

Trust is a major issue for all people, and especially for adults abused as children. They have difficulty trusting their own reactions, thoughts, feelings, and perceptions. Trust is basic to human relationships, and its absence makes finding and keeping friends and lovers difficult, if not impossible.

When one cannot trust, a vicious cycle begins. The less you trust, the less likely you are to have friends or intimate relationships. The more isolated you become, the less you *can* trust others. When others do not seek you out, or you cannot seem to make friends, you may think that there is something wrong with you. Thus you feel more vulnerable, and more in need of guarding yourself rather than trusting enough to be open. (Remember the wall?)

It is easy to understand why trust becomes a major issue for adults abused as children when you remember that trust is learned in childhood. As children, we were totally dependent upon our parents. We trusted that they would feed us, change our diapers, keep us safe and warm. When this trust is unknown or broken, it is difficult to restore.

29

*"If sometimes when you cried you got
fed, and sometimes you got beaten..."*

If when you cried, sometimes you were fed, and
sometimes you were beaten, you cannot develop
trust or learn to expect consistent nurturing
responses. You either learn to stop crying, or take a
risk each time and see what happens. To stay safe,
most adults abused as children stopped taking
chances, and expected little from others. To change
these behaviors, you must begin to take risks slowly,
but purposefully, by giving yourself the opportunity
to test your trust with trustworthy people.

DIFFICULTIES WITH SELF-PROTECTION

"I can take care of myself — nothing hurts."

"If someone you know constantly comes up to you and takes a punch at your face..."

If someone you know constantly comes up to you and takes a punch at your face, when that person comes near you, you put your arms up to block the swing. You have learned to respond in this protective way.

One way to protect yourself is by not needing or wanting anything. If you expect nothing, you cannot be disappointed. And, if you don't want or need anything, you can avoid abusive reactions to your needs.

You may have protected yourself by being extremely good and cooperative, never getting dirty, never speaking unless spoken to, or being *"seen and not heard"*. If you were physically or sexually abused, you may have learned to *"turn off"* body pain or sensations. You may have gone *"into a trance"* when being beaten or sexually abused to protect yourself from the pain. These were survival skills that helped you stay safe. You may not need these skills anymore.

DIFFICULTIES WITH SELF-ESTEEM
"Do I have anything to offer?"

Self-esteem is your sense of who you are. Do you have something to say? Do you have something to offer? Are you loveable? Adults abused as children often see themselves as worthless, crazy, or bad people who have nothing valuable to say or contribute.

I am bad

Most abused children grow up thinking they are bad. There is a simple explanation for this. In the world of the child, to be hurt means that he or she is bad. Children need to isolate and identify this badness in themselves and others to explain and understand it. Children will frequently find the badness within themselves rather than their parents, whom they long for and love.

If abused children were to see their parents as bad, they would be jeopardizing their most important relationship. Since they see themselves as extensions of their parents, accepting parents as bad also inevitably means accepting themselves as bad.

Some parents who abuse their children repeatedly tell the children they are bad, no good, and useless. If you were told repeatedly that you were bad and would end up nowhere, you might eventually believe it. You might start acting in ways that support that belief.

Children who are abused tend to make very rigid divisions or splits in the way they think or view people and issues. Things are either all good or all bad. When they see themselves as all bad, they convince themselves that the parents are all good. They defend their parents and refuse to acknowledge any wrong-doing on their part. As abused children grow up, they may view themselves as bad, and everybody else as good, or, at least better. On the other hand, some abused children can see themselves as good, and others bad. They can become afraid of others and avoid them for fear of getting hurt. In its extreme form, these people can expect only pain and suffering from others, and see everyone as a potential attacker.

Some children who are abused come up with another way of protecting themselves. They become *"tough,"* aggressive, and hostile when relating to others. Other children seek *"gang-identification"* to feel powerful, and gain safety in numbers. Still other children become overweight, or cover themselves up with extra clothing. They believe if they keep to themselves (hide themselves), no one will bother them or pick on them. Unfortunately, this *"different"* behavior sometimes encourages other kids to pick on them, and this further reinforces the belief that ***"there is something wrong with me."***

*"However, if you use some of
these same ways of protecting ..."*

Finally, another common way that people protect
themselves is by not speaking or making eye contact.
Hair or dark glasses which hide the face, and silence,
can be equally effective. You can train people not to

expect anything from you if everytime they speak to you, you answer *"yes"* or *"no"*, and then look at the floor. Protecting yourself when you were a child was appropriate. It helped you survive. But these same behaviors as an adult *separate* you from others, make you feel bad, and keep you from getting what you want. Techniques you learned as a child can outgrow their usefulness and new ones must be learned. You also need to learn that you do not need to protect yourself from everyone. ***Detecting real danger, rather than having a reflex reaction to potential or assumed danger, is a skill to be learned and developed.***

I am unworthy/unloveable

Adults abused as children may feel worthless and unloveable. They may think to themselves, *"If my own parents thought I was no good, how can anyone else think differently?"* Because they frequently don't expect much from others, they make few, if any, demands. They often cannot identify their needs or are unable to articulate them.

The *"bad"* aspects of yourself may have been emphasized for so long that you have slowly been convinced they are *all* you are.If you meet someone you like, you may automatically assume s/he will not like you, or would certainly like someone else better. You may think *"They couldn't possibly be interested in me ... I have nothing to offer."*

Even though you may have felt that way up to now, you can change your opinion of yourself. And, once you change your mind about yourself, others may join you. The first step is to emphasize the positive aspects of yourself. Ask yourself, *"what qualities or talents do I have that are admirable and worthwhile?" "What do I like about myself?"* At first, you may not be able to find one positive thing about yourself, but with practice, you will be surprised at how many strengths you can find when you dare to see.

DIFFICULTIES WITH ACHIEVEMENT

By now you can see how many different reactions you may have to being abused. Another area of difficulty is achieving success and being satisfied once you have reached your goals. Some adults abused as children feel pressure to outperform everybody else. They believe that they must try harder and work harder because they are not as good. They may feel driven and obsessed.

Even when they have clearly succeeded, adults abused as children may still feel they have not done enough or that someone could have done it better.

Other adults abused as children do the opposite: they believe they can accomplish nothing, so they don't try. They hold themselves back from taking chances because it is safer. Since success often makes one more important and visible to others, and since visibility is associated with being hurt, success means danger.

DIFFICULTIES WITH FITTING IN

Children who grow up being put down, held back, beaten, taken advantage of, ignored, and misused or maltreated, find it hard to trust, and expect little from others except pain. They protect themselves by staying isolated and may frequently feel that as long as they don't have to relate to anyone else, they will manage. Loneliness may become a way of life for

*"These adults can overwhelm
other people..."*

these children. An abused child often plays alone, makes friends only with a pet, or creates a rich fantasy life.

If you were abused as a child, you may find yourself an outsider in many social situations. You may not know how to approach people. You may feel pressured to say the *"right"* thing. You may be very nervous about saying the wrong thing. Because you are so careful about what you say, you may give others the impression that you have nothing to say or are not interested in them. They may think that *they* are making you uncomfortable, and will shy away. You are left feeling that your worst fears have come true ...*"No one likes me."* You may find yourself having few if any friends, and those you do have may be one-sided. You do for them, and little comes back.

But this is not the only way abused children relate to others. Another possible reaction is very different. A person may attach him or herself to anyone who is halfway friendly or interested, and is deeply disappointed when the friendship is not returned in kind. This adult wants desperately to be liked, and may cling to others which results in making others feel that they can never give enough. Such behavior can overwhelm other people with needs that are impossible to fulfill. An example would be calling others on the phone three and four times a day, dropping by their homes or jobs, and just generally making others the center of your attention. You may feel you *"cannot stand"* to be away from the loved person, and seek them out excessively, eliciting their rejection.

There is a middle road in which you don't hold back or push forward too much. That's the road to be explored.

DIFFICULTIES WITH INTIMATE RELATIONSHIPS

Adults abused as children have had little experience loving and being loved in a safe way from those first very important people, their parents. They have usually received inconsistent affection or caring. They may have grown up believing that abuse is a sign of love. *"If someone loves me, they hit me,"* or *"if they care, they show you by having sex with you."* This hitting or sexually abusive behavior can be seen as an alternative to no contact. Many children have said that at least when they were abused, they knew they were *"real"* and had some value to their parents. Sexually abused children may feel that their abuse kept the family together, and in that sense they learned you sacrifice and endure the pain when you love.

Neglected or abused children have sometimes never been touched, held, caressed, or nurtured in appropriate ways. When touched now by potential lovers or affectionate friends, they may flinch, pull away, or tighten their muscles. They don't know how to respond to a touch that does not hurt or intrude.

Some children learned to disconnect their emotional reactions from their bodily reactions. Physically

40

abused children may have learned not to cry or complain because that got them into more trouble. Some sexually abused children can describe the ceilings in their rooms in great detail because while the abuse happened, they focused on something else waiting for it to be over. Being sexually abused has many implications in adult intimate relationships which include sexual expression. The issue of body safety and potential rejection will usually surface. Sexuality and sexual contacts can trigger memories and reactions that are unpleasant and interfere with trusting others and developing intimate relationships.

"If someone loves me, they hit me."

Adults sexually or physically abused as children may find themselves avoiding intimate relationships out of fear or discomfort. To make matters more complicated, these adults will sometimes enter relationships with mates who eventually beat them, mistreat them, and emotionally abuse them. In other words, they repeat their childhood experiences, and are revictimized. The outsider may conclude, *"that person is a glutton for punishment."*

"Adults sexually or physically abused as children may find themselves avoiding..."

Two very important concepts help us understand this pattern of repeating a painful past. First, if someone has a choice between a familiar (comfortable) situation or feeling, and an unfamiliar (uncomfortable) situation or feeling, s/he will usually choose the former. It is safer, and elicits less anxiety because it is a known.

Secondly, sometimes the adult abused as a child unconsciously chooses the familiar abusive situation in order to recreate the old scene and come to terms with it. There is a desire to see if this time s/he can make it stop or try to understand better why the original abuse occurred in the first place.

Like everyone else, adults abused as children have learned over the years to react in certain ways. These responses are difficult to change, even if they are understood as undesirable. The pattern of being involved in abusive relationships takes a lot of time and perseverance to break, but it can be broken by taking small steps towards clear goals.

Another pattern that might prevent finding or keeping a satisfying mate is when the original victim (the abused child) becomes the aggressor (the abusive adult). When children are beaten or watch their parents beat, ignore, or mistreat each other, they learn both roles - aggressor and victim. The child can later assume either position. **This abusive behavior often surfaces in intimate relationships because it was learned in that context, and other tools**

for resolving conflict (such as negotiating, com-
promising, problem solving) have not yet been
learned or practiced.

chapter five

PATTERNS OF RELATING
TO THE WORLD

Caretaker/Rescuer

Some adults abused as children develop very effective care-taking skills. They see themselves as capable of unconditional love. Some join the helping professions and make excellent daycare workers, babysitters, workers in senior citizen homes, waitresses, doctors, nurses, social workers, therapists, etc. They give to others what they wish to receive themselves. They often set up an impossible situation however, by giving so well that no one could possibly return in kind. They burn themselves out, and sometimes end up resenting those to whom they are giving. Such behavior is often fuelled by the unconscious fantasy, *"If I serve, I will get what I never had and always wanted"*. Giving needs to be balanced with receiving.

The *"caretaker"* and *"the rescuer"* always find troubled people to help. Rescuers may do extreme things like letting people move into their homes without rent, and they may generally greatly inconvenience themselves. They give at their own expense. But they do not allow others to give to them. Rescuers may encourage dependency, while insisting that they want nothing in return. It often ends in resentment.

"They also wear themselves down, and sometimes end up resenting those whom they serve."

Hider

A hider is someone who tries hard not to be noticed. S/he may hide physically by being too thin, too fat, too non-descript, or by staying home. This person may *"mask"* his or her face with hair, glasses, or lots of makeup and especially avoids those contacts which might become explosive (violent).

Take me, I'm yours.

Boundaries are the invisible lines that people draw to control closeness and distance. They are the spoken and unspoken rules that define the expectations and limits of specific kinds of relationships. For example, certain family members (brothers, sisters, parents, and children) do not have sex with each other.

Therapists do not socialize or have affairs with their clients.

In families where abuse occurs, the boundaries are often vague and confused. A father who is distant and/or upset with his wife may want his daughter to take her place in every way. This violates the father-daughter boundary; the father then asks the daughter to meet needs that should be handled by the mother or other adults. If you grew up in a home with unclear or inconsistent rules, there was no opportunity to learn these boundaries and their rules. People expected too much or too little from you, and you may not know how to regulate the boundaries of current relationships.

If you have difficulties either setting and keeping boundaries in your relationships, you are either letting others make unreasonable demands, you are expecting too much from others, or you are giving too much. Setting limits will help protect you from both being used and/or disappointed by others.

I'm Tough, Nothing Hurts Me

When individuals assume the role of *"tough guy"*, they numb the pain in order to get through the day. They may drink heavily or take drugs to *"pad"* themselves from unpleasantness. They may be oblivious to their surroundings. When people drink or use drugs, they numb themselves to everything and experience less pain, but also less sadness, fear, excitement, motivation, and affection. Some people use food as *"padding"*. Stuffing food into your mouth can appease or postpone pain, but such addictive behaviors do not solve problems, and frequently cause their own.

Lost Souls

Many adults abused as children lack direction or *"roots"*. They float about unable to connect to other people, to secure jobs, or create permanent homes. They are frequently in flight, and always seem confused about their next step. This activity prevents them from setting goals.

Walking Time-Bombs

"... so close to the surface it is as if the bomb will explode at the slightest provocation ..."

Many adults abused as children understandably carry a lot of anger inside them. This anger is sometimes controlled, but lies so close to the surface that it can explode at the slightest provocation. These individuals are often negative and hostile and are prone to pick fights. They seem to anticipate an eventual battle, and want to take control by creating or precipitating conflict. Their motto is *"The best defense is a good offense."* They may simply never have learned to channel anger appropriately. Instead, they are overwhelmed by it. These angry adults, morally outraged by the wrongs or injustices of life, may join many *"causes"* and identify with retaliatory behaviors such as vigilantism and non-peaceful demonstrations.

The Only Thing That Helps is Dying

Some abused children think a great deal about being invisible and dying. They may think, *"I can't take it anymore; I can't make it stop."* They feel helpless, overpowered, and afraid of the abuse happening again. Their reality is painful. They may wish themselves or their abusers dead. These frightened children may entertain suicidal escape thoughts. They believe that they don't deserve to live. This feeling of unworthiness or emptiness can easily slip into a death wish. If these thoughts remain secret and unresolved, adults abused as children may try to act on these wishes. They see suicide as control over their lives. If you find yourself constantly visiting cemeteries, going to morose movies, reading about darkness and death, physically cutting or hurting yourself, or planning ways to kill yourself or others,

TALK TO SOMEONE ABOUT THESE THOUGHTS, FEELINGS, AND BEHAVIORS. SEEK PROFESSIONAL HELP IMMEDIATELY. THERE ARE ALTERNATIVES TO DEATH!

My Head Aches, Hug Me

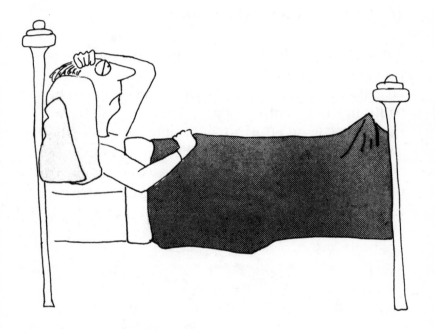

Some adults abused as children who are unable to cope with their memories or who cannot express unspoken secrets, wishes, or fears, may feel overwhelmed. Sometimes they internalize this stress making themselves physically sick. They may also be accident prone. Through sickness and pain, their bodies express what they cannot verbalize. Illness may pay off with a trip to the doctor or special attention from friends and acquaintances. Why this behavior? There are a couple of explanations. Some abused children have brief loving reunions with remorseful parents after the beatings. They learn to expect rewards after pain. Others may have cried out for help by getting a medical examination. Still others think that asking for caretaking when ill is the only time to make emotional demands or requests.

If it hurts, I know I'm here

Some abused children interpret pain as a familiar expression of parental love or attention. They may, in fact, take a knife or sharp object and cut themselves badly in the parent's absence. They may be hurting themselves in an effort to be symbolically near their abusive parent, connecting to them in a familiar way. Or self-mutilation may occur to reassure them that they can still feel and are alive. These self-destructive tendencies are dangerous and must be stopped.

chapter six

TAKING HOLD OF YOUR PAST

There are good reasons for **not** changing. Making changes of any kind is hard work. It is usually easier to stay the way you've always been. When you make a change, especially in an important area of your life, such as relating to others, you take risks. For example, it might be safer to stay home and not go to a party than go to the party and feel nervous about making conversation or worrying about your appearance. It might be easier to hide and keep your feelings to yourself rather than to risk being visible and thus vulnerable to feared attacks.

It's important to recognize that until now, you have probably had good reasons for **not** changing. Think for a minute of something you want to change. Now think hard of all the disadvantages of doing so. You probably can list many after-effects that might be scary.

Until now, you have been protecting yourself from real or imagined harm. You have been expecting others to dislike you, disappoint you, or hurt you.

It will take time and perseverance to break those thought patterns and replace them with positive ones. You will frequently be discouraged and wonder if it's worth the effort; however, push yourself to try again. You will see progress even if it's slow initially.

Once a Victim, Always a Victim?

Adults abused as children struggle with the question, *"Will I ever recover?" "Will I ever lead a normal life?"* They may feel hopeless about making lasting changes finding that their positive resolutions fizzle out quickly. These adults may feel *"damaged"* for life. But, as mentioned previously, changes can occur, and they take time. It is important to be patient with yourself and take credit for your progress.

"Remember, the journey of a thousand miles begins with a single step."

You may want to take a very small risk, test it out, and then retreat for a while. Imagine yourself as a young child again who is deciding whether or not to take a first step. First you stand, then sit again. Then you stand, try a small step, and sit. Pleased with yourself and confident, you try some more. Life is a series of standing, sitting, falling, and taking little steps. When you were learning to walk, you may have done it near a wall, so you could hold on with one hand. You may have held someone's hand to steady yourself. You may find it difficult to accept support for the changes you want to make at this time in your life. A therapist, or others who were also abused, may be of great help during this transition period. Remember **the journey of a thousand miles starts with a single step.**

Once a Victim, Now an Abuser?

Some adults abused as children nervously react to the child abuse information that states, *"Most abusive parents were themselves abused as children."* They may fear that they are **destined** to beat their own children. Many abused children grow up to be non-abusive parents, or successful adults who choose not to have children.

Some adults abused as children do become aggressors. They learned well the lessons of violence: *"You hurt the ones you love,"* and *"Violence solves problems."* They may find themselves unable to control their anger, or need to appear *"tough,"* *"strong,"* or *"as bad as the next guy."* In an attempt to *"even the score,"* they seek out victims. Or, by acting out the role of the abuser, they may be unconsciously trying to understand why the earlier

56

abuse occurred — *"I love my wife and hit her -maybe my dad loved my mom and hit her."*

"Once a victim, now an abuser?"

Violence is learned. It can be controlled. New lessons can be learned about safe and effective ways of relating or resolving conflicts.

Nothing Matters Anymore - Why Try?

Some adults abused as children may feel that they cannot change. They simply give up and throw in the towel. Let me repeat that not changing is a form of self-protection. If nothing is ventured, you remain safe. These adults are understandably exhausted. Their ability to comply was an important survival skill - *"Don't object, don't complain, sit there and take it."* They may also feel deeply depressed and have feelings of extreme deprivation. They may not have the interpersonal skills necessary to build or sustain satisfying relationships. They may be afraid to hope. When motivation is replaced by apathy, this person can benefit from therapy. The therapist may recommend a regimen of activity both to rekindle interest in life, and to change the unrewarding behavior patterns.

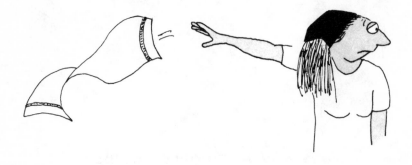

Becoming Whole: No More Splitting

Most adults abused as children have a well-defined sense of their badness, and little appreciation for their positive side. They judge their weaknesses very harshly, and rarely take credit for, or even identify, their strengths. The balanced individual can accept both negative and positive.

The negative *"bad"* side of you was probably emphasized for years. It is as if your imperfect, *"bad"* side was a plant that was watered, put in the sun, nurtured, talked to, and grew to full capacity. Meanwhile, the plant in the shade, the *"good"* you, was ignored, and therefore could not thrive.

"Another way to think of yourself is in terms of both strengths and weaknesses."

YOU ARE NOT A CHILD IN THE PRESENT AND YOU CANNOT RELIVE THE PAST. Your parents may not be physically present to any great extent in your life now, or they may be in the same abusive roles they always had. They may be unwilling or unable to establish a positive relationship with you. So it's up to you to nurture yourself and stop waiting for them to change. Begin by identifying and discovering your strengths. Give yourself full credit for what you do well; you deserve it.

Imagine how you would like to be talked to or treated. Then, play that scene out in your imagination. Seek out people who treat you well, who respect and support you. Develop those friendships. Let them help you by telling them what you need. Take small risks at first. Don't rush yourself. If you find that you are constantly berating yourself for something that you did not do perfectly, counter that by identifying something you did well. (So you burned the rice; the vegetables were just right.) Balance yourself out. Give yourself credit.

I predict that you will have an easy time finding your faults. I challenge you to find your hidden, or unexpressed talents, to recognize and take pride in your accomplishments, and remember them when you make a mistake or do something badly. Don't let mistakes set you back. **Everyone** makes them. **No one** is perfect.

Once you can accept both the positives and negatives of yourself, you are well on your way to feeling more whole. You will experience greater balance and fewer dramatic mood swings. Your confidence may grow. You will then be less likely to be hard on yourself.

Constructive Anger Expression

If you feel angry a lot of the time, you are not unusual. If you can express or channel constructively your angry thoughts and feelings, you are unusual. Most of us do not learn to express our anger in *"ac-*

ceptable" ways. Our culture frowns on the expression of anger. Children's anger is usually seen as bad or unacceptable. Temper tantrums are often punished. Anger is not inherently bad. Expressing it violently is.

No one can tell you how to express your anger safely, but exploring the question is important. You may want to talk to your friends, therapist, or others about this issue. How do they handle their anger? Some people engage in physical activity since anger shows itself in the body by making tight, tense muscles. Running, jogging, and other forms of exercising can release energy and cool you down. Some people take showers, talk to friends, stomp on egg cartons, or punch pillows. Other people meditate and find ways of relaxing their bodies like taking hot baths or getting massaged.

"Some people jog, take a shower..."

It is also crucial to look at what makes you angry and develop tools for problem solving, resolving conflict, setting limits, and communicating effectively. Avoid anger *"build-ups"* by keeping in touch with your feelings.

As mentioned previously, anger is usually the flip-side of helplessness. You may want to ask yourself, *"What do I feel helpless about and how can I regain some power or control?"* rather than, *"What am I angry about?"*

Respond, Don't React

If you've been hit, you may understandably fear attacks. If you've been molested or raped, it's hard to trust it won't happen again. If you've been neglected, it's difficult to imagine anyone caring about your welfare.

Even in a safe environment, the instinct to protect oneself may continue to operate although it is no longer vitally necessary. This spontaneous behavior or reaction can actually be counter-productive at this point in your life. Learning new responses will be important.

It is more useful to **respond** to others, rather than to react. When you are responsive, you have noticed the reflex, but you have paused to take some time to evaluate your thoughts and feelings, and you have measured the consequences of taking specific actions.

When you are responsive rather than reactive, you usually have thought through what you really want to accomplish and may present yourself in a way that contributes to a useful exchange. When you are responsive, others tend to listen and cooperate.

Create Opportunities

It is useful to think of past abuse in this way: It happened, it was painful, it cannot be undone. It has predisposed you to certain vulnerabilities, but you can make positive changes. You survived the abuse by developing good survival skills. You now need to replace those protective skills with responsive behaviors.

It is not enough to understand why you may be shy, get threatened, or tolerate abusive relationships; you must now create opportunities for change. How?

You begin by taking small risks and chances. That is the only way you will get new information about yourself and others. Speak to someone you might not ordinarily approach. Tell them something about yourself. Ask them about themselves. Many people like to talk about personal things.

Try to believe that the nice things someone says about your are accurate. Learn to accept compliments. Call a friend you haven't seen for a while and ask if s/he would like to do something together. If s/he says no try again.

In some cases, adults abused as children tell strangers and acquaintances about their abuse, only to find that people shy away, or worse, tell them they were to blame. This may happen because many people feel uncomfortable with other people's pain, and do not know how to respond. I encourage you to find other things to talk about at first: a movie you saw, an article you read in the newspaper, one of your hobbies or interests. If you have none, now is a great time to develop one.

If you have always had a secret wish, there is no better time than now to pursue it. Perhaps you've always wanted to see the inside of a bowling alley, go to a baseball game, listen to live music, or roller skate in the park. Arrange to do just that. Many adults abused as children missed part of their childhood. Now is the time to recapture some of it by doing fun *"childish"* things. Go ahead, you deserve it.

Some people may not be able to define *"fun"* or identify with fun activities. Make a list of things you wonder about, and start trying them out. Allow yourself to enjoy yourself. With this kind of exploration, you can begin to make connections with the world. This sense of connectedness will help you gain your balance and feel like part of life. The sensation of floating and drifting can disappear as you begin to find yourself — who you really are, not who you were told you were, or grew up to think you were.

Get Free of Familiar Traps

Adults abused as children are influenced by their beliefs about themselves, such as *"People will not like me," "People will laugh at how I look,"* or *"Everyone is better than me."* These are old tapes that repeat in your mind. It doesn't take long to start believing them.

Other people have different tapes. They think, *"Everyone thinks I'm great," "I'm the best looking person in the world,"* or *"I'm superior."* **They may feel just as insecure inside, but have different external responses.** If you put two people with these two different kinds of beliefs about themselves together, they are a perfect match. They complement each other. Each supports, reinforces, and shares responsibility in the interaction. The person who feels superior will try to control the person who feels inferior. The person who feels inferior may feel terrorized or victimized by the apparently stronger person who demands obedience. Both stay in control of the outcome by their contribution to the interaction. If you are the inferior-feeling person, you may feel inadequate, especially in the company of the superior-feeling person. That person supports your negative self-picture and is therefore comfortable and familiar. The superior-feeling person may also feel inadequate since it takes so much effort to avoid facing the truth - s/he also feels insecure and inferior.

It can be helpful to acknowledge your vulnerabilities, but avoid those people who seem to support your weaknesses and discourage your strengths.

Try to present yourself in such a way that others are not as aware of your vulnerable, sensitive areas. For example, if you are nervous around your boss and find that you cannot speak when s/he is near, notice your nervous behavior. Do you avoid eye contact, mumble, shift weight from one foot to the other? Try to change those responses. Make eye contact, even if for short periods of time ... look at her or his nose if the eyes are particularly hard. Try sitting down when you speak to him or her. Try speaking in a regular voice, slowly, but clearly.

As you make these changes, you will gain more self confidence and you will see firsthand that nothing bad happens. As a matter of fact, you might find your boss suddenly behaving in a more positive way towards you.

Pratice speaking to your boss in front of a mirror. Take turns exaggerating your nervousness and how you think you might look, and then change to a more in-control presentation of yourself. Practice looking in the eyes of people you feel comfortable with. Let others know you are nervous. Sometimes just saying you are nervous helps. Other people usually understand, since everyone feels nervous at one time or another. Stay clear of familiar traps. Remember, small steps mean forward movement. As long as you keep moving, change can occur.

Become Visible

If you were abused as a child, you learned survival skills. They were necessary then because they kept you alive, or helped *"pad"* you from the pain. However, a real threat may not be present now in your life, and those skills are no longer necessary

One such skill was learning to be invisible. Many adults abused as children became experts. They learned to stand still, hold their breath, leave the room, or blend in with the furniture so as not to provoke an attack. They learned to avoid being hit, berated with words, or sexually assaulted or misused by being emotionally or physically distant or disconnected.

Being emotionally disconnected is a survival skill that kept you from feeling intense pain. For example, a child who is sexually abused may fill her or his mind with other thoughts during the abuse or pretend to be asleep. The child spares him/herself pain by disconnecting and imagining that the abuse is not happening, or happening to someone else.

The problem with being emotionally disconnected in relation to the rest of the world is that often, in addition to not feeling pain, little else is felt. Positive, loving feelings, if any are available, are also screened out.

This skill, in adult life, hinders the individual's ability to trust, to experience a broad range of emotions, and to form and sustain satisfying relationships. It is important to let go of survival skills that are no longer necessary.

Know Your Own Power

If you were abused as a child, you probably grew up feeling powerless to stop the abuse, or to change anything at all. As a youngster, you had limited power, both physically and emotionally.

As an adult, it is important to recognize your own power. Two reactions seem to commonly occur. One is a real fear of overwhelming others with the intensity of strong feelings. Hence, this power must be kept tightly reined in. Sometimes this results in ineffective actions with others, and you may be left feeling powerless to make positive changes by holding back too much. The other reaction is overwhelming others in order to make a point or change something. The goal may be accomplished, but at the expense of personal disapproval from others. It is neither necessary to *"hold back"* entirely nor to overcome someone with your power. There is a middle ground. You might find it useful to experiment using a little of your power at a time until you discover the balance which gets you the best results.

Adults abused as children seek to regain power in many ways. One way is by intellectualizing, trying to impress others by using words that no one understands, or appearing to know all the answers. When you talk all the time, you probably fear that if you stop, someone may say something you don't want to hear. Or if you stop talking, the other person will leave. You might also talk non-stop to cover the anxiety you feel when you are with others.

Both intellectualizing and talking too much are ways to exert power or feel in control. They can also create distance between you and others. If this happens, the over-talking is not working for you since your goal is to become more connected to people.

Another way of being in control is by being psychologically minded and trying to analyze past events. When these individuals speak, it is as if they were telling a story that happened to someone else. Again, they have learned to disconnect from the pain, and in doing so, feel less pain and upset. It is important to deal with the old pain so it does not interfere with making positive contact with others.

Broaden Your Possibilities

It is worth repeating that if you were abused, you had limited options. You could cry, hide, stick your tongue out, disconnect from body sensations, eat a lot, not eat, hurt yourself, get sick, etc. As an adult, you have more possibilities. Remember this when you feel dissatisfied with the way you handled a situation and think of other ways you could have behaved or other things you could have said. Consider how other people might have reacted to different responses from you.

chapter seven

SAY GOODBYE
TO THE PARENTS
YOU NEVER HAD

As long as you continue to pine for what never was, and never can be, you are stuck in the past.

If you were abused, you missed the safe, consistent loving experience every child deserves. You were never encouraged to develop self-confidence and a sense of belonging and worth. You must say good-bye to the *"wish"* for perfect parents and continue with the rest of your life. It will be hard for you since you are not yet sure what's available and possible. Small chances and risks will give you new information to consider. What kind of contact with people feels good? What is it like to have a conversation with someone who is interested in you? What are feelings of closeness like? How and when do you feel safe with others? **When you give up the wish for the parents you hoped for, you make room for the real people in your life.**

In addition to giving up the wish, you must also say good-bye to the ghosts of the parents you did have. They can invade your thoughts and interfere with your current relationships. As safe as you may feel in familiar abusive relationships, you must slowly venture out into the unfamiliar and tolerate the anxiety of the unknown.

When speaking with adults abused as children about their parents or families, the question is always raised about what to do with the knowledge or acceptance of abuse at this point.

This is a very complicated question with no clear-cut answers. My advice is this: If you are going to *"confront"* your parents about the abuse, make sure that you have no specific outcomes in mind since you may be setting yourself up for deep disappointment. Some formerly abused children long for their parent's *"confession"* (admission of responsibility) and their plea for forgiveness. Do not expect this. It is frequently beyond the reach of parents who may have struggled all their lives to deny or cover-up the abuse. Some abusive parents will deny the events completely, and turn on you once again, implying that you are sick, crazy, or disturbed to make such an accusation. Your fantasy of getting a long-deserved apology or some effort at compensation or comfort may be quickly dispelled.

An already strained, weak relationship with parents may totally break down as a result of confrontation. Be aware of this possibility. If you are ready to face it, take the chance. If you might be devestated by the denial or accusatory response, take more time before acting. Some adults abused as children have gained support and comfort from parents who have regretted their actions, were not aware of the extent and impact of their behavior on the child, or were in a situation where one parent did not know the other one was being abusive. In general, however, such understanding is the exception rather than the rule when adults abused as children confront their families.

Say Hello to the Parent You Can Be If You Choose

Many adults abused as children fear having children. They may have heard that most abusive parents were abused children. While this is true, there are many abused children who become capable, nurturing parents. Sometimes they had a significant person in their lives who modeled good parenting. In other instances, counseling helped them put their pasts into perspective.

"Say hello to the parents you can be."

We are fortunate to live in a time and culture which support parents getting the help they need or want. Parents are no longer expected to know *"instinctively"* how to handle their kids, and they are not rejected for seeking assistance. Parent groups, parenting classes, and telephone hotlines are ready, willing, and able to discuss parenting. Do not deny yourself the experience of being a parent because you fear you will repeat the abusive pattern. Discuss your specific concerns, fears, and wishes with a counselor or other adults abused as children.

Rescuing Yourself: No More Pipe Dreams

As an abused child, you may have waited in vain for someone to come and rescue you. As an adult, you may still be looking for solutions outside yourself: *"If only the job were better," "If only people understood me," "I wish I had someone to take care of me."*

It is more productive to look to yourself for these answers and solutions, for your own sense of safety and accomplishment. Relying on others can result in disappointment. It fosters your dependence on the presence and protection of others to feel safe, which can fuel the pattern of clinging and overwhelming others with your needs. The strength to take the steps will come from you with perhaps a little help from your friends. Learning how to venture out and take risks while protecting yourself from unnecessary hurts build your confidence and trust. These are important lessons for everyone, but particularly difficult for someone whose painful past experiences haunt him or her.

ADDENDUM

The Non-Abused Sibling

In cases of physical violence, neglect, emotional or sexual abuse, all family members may be affected.

If you were a non-abused child in your family, it is likely you had one or more of the following reactions:

Guilt: Some of you may have felt guilty that you were not the child receiving the abuse. You may feel that you **should** have protested, or in some way helped your brother or sister. You probably felt helpless about stopping the abuse, but in retrospect may feel responsible for not making more of an effort.

You may have also felt relieved that you were not abused. At the same time, you may have felt guilty for reacting in this manner. Some of you may have tried to provoke abuse from a parent or caretaker on occassion to "prove" your loyalty to your sibling.

Fear: Even though you may not have been the child singled out for abuse, you may have lived in fear that someday the tide would change, and you would have to suffer from a beating, emotional or sexual abuse, or parental rejection. Some siblings are made to "witness" what happens to bad children, and these types of warnings are frequently terrifying.

Promoting yourself as the "perfect" child: In an effort to avoid getting abused, you may have made efforts to be seen as the "good" child, seeking to stay in your parent's good graces. This was a normal "adaptive" reaction to the situation, but you may now feel guilty and ashamed that you behaved in this manner.

The non-abused child, like the abused child, may carry the memories and pain into adulthood and may look back and make judgements on his/her behavior. It is crucial for the non-abused sibling to understand that evaluating the past from an adult's point of view necessarily includes adult realizations. Children do not have the abilities and choices adults do.

The greatest tragedy for the non-abused sibling is that their guilt may prevent them from maintaining contact with their abused sibling. Both need assistance in "working through" their feelings and reactions to each other, but once that is accomplished it is possible to build a familial relationship of mutual benefit.

Partners of Adults Abused as Children

As noted earlier in the book, adults abused as children may have a variety of long-term reactions to their childhood abuse. It is often difficult for them to start or keep long-lasting satisfying relationships. Often the spouse or partner of the adult abused as a child has many feelings and reactions which can assist or interfere with building and sustaining the relationship.

The Rescuer: Sometimes, when the abused adult recounts their history, those around them may feel an overwhelming desire to protect the person, and provide a totally different experience for them. This may become an unrealistic desire, since all relationships include struggling, conflict, and stress.

Partners of adults abused as children may set themselves up to fail, if they expect they can "make up" for the abuse, by becoming parent, lover, friend, and rescuer. Afraid to repeat the abuse, they may go to the other extreme, overly-protecting the adult abused as a child.

The unwitting punisher: Often, the adult abused as a child, may feel uncomfortable with the all-loving partner, and may from time to time behave in such a way as to provoke the kind of abuse she/he learned growing up. They are not trying to get abused, they are trying to get comfortable, by re-creating a familiar situation. The partner may suddenly find him/herself having rageful or hateful feelings towards the adult abused as a child, and may feel a great deal of guilt and pain about this reaction. It is important to notice if this situation begins to occur, and nip it at the bud by talking about it, or seeking help.

Confusion: An adult abused as a child has not had the role-modeling of what a positive adult relationship is like. Because of this, they may flounder around, trying to find how to relate on a day to day basis to someone they love. This behavior can be confusing to a partner, who may feel rejected, accepted, and challenged constantly. The confusion can lead to frustration and even resentment. Again, these are feelings that can serve as signals to notice and talk about the situation.

Helplessness, Pain and Anger: Partners of adults abused as children, may feel a large sense of pain for what those they loved have endured. Frequently, they must maintain relationships with in-laws, knowing full well the abuse that occurred in the past. While the adult abused as a child may have his/her own way of relating to their family, the partner may feel helpless to change anything, and respectful of his partner's wishes, may not confront or acknowledge the past.

This feeling of helplessness will of course create a sense of anger which may not always be expressed directly.

Impatience: Partners of adults abused as children may feel impatient with their mate's struggles around the abuse in their childhood. They may feel that the past is the past, and may frequently find themselves irritated at the attention directed away from the present and the relationship. This may make partners feel insensitive and guilty.

This is a shorthand version of some of the issues I believe can affect the non-abused sibling and the partners of adults abused as children. I hope if you fall into one of these categories that you will see yourself as worthy of assistance in dealing the indirect impact of child abuse.

Epilogue

After reading this book, you may have a better sense of whether or not you were abused as a child. Hopefully, you have also acknowledged the impact of this experience on some of your thoughts and feelings about yourself and people in your life.

This has been a good first step. I hope that now you will continue in the process of putting the experiences in perspective and making positive changes in your life.

There are many people and organizations willing to help. Counselors in many areas have started groups for adults physically, sexually, or emotionally abused as children, and individual therapists are also available if the idea of a group sounds too scary. There are also self-help groups, hotlines, and other resources which you may find useful. In the next few pages, I am giving you some references for more reading material, as well as resources you can call to get additional information.

Congratulations on finishing the book and good luck with your journey.

Eliana

National Resources

*To find resources in your area, call of write to these National Organizations:

Parents Anonymous
22330 Hawthorne Blvd., Suite 208
Torrance, CA 90505 (800) 352-0386

Parents United/Sons and Daughters United
(sexual abuse treatment)
P. O. Box 952
San Jose, CA 95108 (408) 280-5055

National Center of Child Abuse and Neglect
  (NCCAN)
Department of Health and Human Services
P. O. Box 1182
Washington, D.C. 20013 (202) 245-2856

National Committee for Prevention of Child Abuse
332 South Michigan Avenue, Suite 1250
Chicago, IL 60604-4357 (312) 663-3520

C. Henry Kempe National Center for the Prevention
  & Treatment of Child Abuse and Neglect
1205 Oneida Street
Denver, CO 80220 (303) 321-3963

*Resources include hotlines, self-help groups, homemaker services, respite care, groups for adults abused as children (survivors), Parents Anonymous (self-help for abusive parents), Parents United (child sexual abuse treatment for families), Child Abuse Councils, and counseling services.

Your local Child Abuse Councils can give you information and referral regarding local services, and can provide educational presentations at your church, community group, school, etc.

Suggested Readings

Helfer, Ray **A Crash Course in Childhood**, 1978, First Evaluation Edition published by Ray E. Helfer, Box 1781, East Lansing, MI 48823.

Butler, S. **Conspiracy of Silence**, New Glide Publications, San Francisco, CA, 1978

Herbruck, Chris **Breaking the Cycle of Child Abuse** Winston Press, Minneapolis, MINN, 1979.